DISCIPLESHIP E✝PLORED

STUDY GUIDE
LEADER'S EDITION

This eight-week course – featuring Bible studies, talks and group discussions – explores Paul's letter to the Philippians and its call to live wholeheartedly for Christ.

It is intended for those beginning the Christian life and those who would like a "refresher". In particular, it's ideal for new Christians who have just completed **Christianity Explored**.

This book is divided into three sections: the first explains how to set up your course, the second trains you to use the course, and the third is your guide each week as you actually run the course.

Welcome to **Discipleship Explored.**

SECTION 1
SETTING UP THE COURSE

SECTION 2
TRAINING NOTES

SECTION 3
STUDY GUIDE

This section is intended for the main course leader – the person responsible for organizing the course and delivering the talks. If you are not the main course leader, go to Section 2: Training Notes.

SECTION 1
SETTING UP THE COURSE

SETTING UP THE COURSE
GETTING STARTED

Discipleship Explored takes you, and those in your care, on a journey into Philippians.

To help your course run smoothly, you will need to consider the following before the course begins:

WHERE WILL YOU MEET?

Try to find a place where you will be able to meet every week at the same time. The important thing is that the environment should help people relax so that they will be encouraged to discuss freely. Sharing a meal together will help with this.

It's ideal if your group can continue to meet in the same place they met for *Christianity Explored*.

To meet in a room at your church can also work well, as it will help participants to feel comfortable in the church building.

WHEN WILL YOU MEET?

Once a week for eight weeks is the time required to complete the course.

When you meet will depend on the type of group you are running. Most people will opt for a mid-week evening, but the material works equally well with, for example, a morning group for young mums, a breakfast group for working people, or as an adult Sunday school.

The structure of each week is simple: a meal, a Bible study, a talk, and a group discussion. You should be able to complete this in 2 hours or less.

Below are the suggested timings for each component of the weekly meetings. You can make sessions shorter or longer depending on your circumstances.

Leaders' prayer meeting	15 minutes
Sharing a meal	25 minutes
Group Discussion 1	30 minutes
Talk	20 minutes
Group Discussion 2	30 minutes

HOW WILL YOU INVITE PEOPLE?

Advertise the course in your church bulletin and during the Sunday services. (One way to do this is by downloading the trailer from www.discipleshipexplored.org)

Explain that *Discipleship Explored* involves refreshments or a meal, a Bible study, a talk, a short discussion and plenty of opportunities to ask questions.

At the end of *Christianity Explored*, participants should be invited to join *Discipleship Explored*. The *Christianity Explored* leaders will know who from their group is ready to go on to *Discipleship Explored* and should be encouraging them to do so.

The beauty of studying Mark's Gospel in *Christianity Explored* is that participants should now be eager to explore another part of God's word. Not only that, but they will also be eager to maintain the friendships they have developed while on the course.

WHO WILL LEAD?

The main course leader will be responsible for delivering eight short talks on Philippians, as well as leading a group of their own through the Bible studies and discussion questions. (It is better for one person to deliver all the talks as this develops rapport and trust between the speaker and the participants.)

Ideally, you will have 2 leaders for every 6 participants. These leaders are responsible for guiding the studies and discussions.

In a mixed group, it is desirable to have both a male and a female leader so that they can deal with pastoral situations appropriately.

Leaders should be Christians who are able to teach, encourage discussion and care for participants. They should be able to teach the Bible faithfully and clearly, and handle pastoral situations with care and sensitivity.

Because THE WEEK AHEAD features studies from all over the Bible, leaders will need to have enough general biblical knowledge to help participants with the studies as necessary.

If possible, ask leaders from *Christianity Explored* to lead their participants through *Discipleship Explored* too. If that is not possible, encourage one of the *Christianity Explored* leaders to meet their group on the first week of *Discipleship Explored* and introduce the group to their new leaders.

WHAT WILL YOU NEED?

Sharing a meal together is a core component of *Discipleship Explored*.

Organize a team of people who are able to prepare and serve food each week. If it is impractical to serve a meal, provide light refreshments (coffee and cake, for example).

Everyone on the course – leaders and participants – will need a Bible. For the sake of clarity, it is important that everyone uses the same version. (The version used throughout the course material is the New International Version.)

If they do not already have one, participants should be given a Bible at the start of the course, preferably one they can take away with them so that they can complete THE WEEK AHEAD studies.

Make sure you have enough copies of the *Study Guide* so that every participant has their own copy, and don't forget pens.

SETTING UP THE COURSE
PREPARING THE TALKS

After the meal and the Bible study the course leader delivers a short talk.

The talks work their way chronologically through Philippians.

WEEK 1	Philippians 1:1–11	Confident in Christ
WEEK 2	Philippians 1:12–26	Living in Christ
WEEK 3	Philippians 1:27 – 2:11	Standing Together in Christ
WEEK 4	Philippians 2:12–30	Transformed by Christ
WEEK 5	Philippians 3:1–9	Righteous in Christ
WEEK 6	Philippians 3:10 – 4:1	Knowing Christ
WEEK 7	Philippians 4:2–9	Rejoicing in Christ
WEEK 8	Philippians 4:10–23	Content in Christ

Each week, before the talk, ask one of the leaders to read the relevant passage out loud. Then the course leader should pray and begin the talk.

This section contains outlines of those talks. (In addition, the website www.discipleshipexplored.org contains audio recordings to help you prepare.)

The outlines give a general structure for the talk. They do not cover every aspect of the passage under discussion, but focus on aspects that are particularly relevant to new Christians. Please study the passage carefully, and make these talks your own by adding your own illustrations and observations. But remember also to keep them relatively short. We recommend 20 minutes as a maximum.

OUTLINE OF TALK 1

CONFIDENT IN CHRIST
PHILIPPIANS 1:1–11

AIM

- To welcome people to the course.

- To explain the term "disciple".

- To explain that our confidence as Christians comes from the certainty that God always finishes the work he starts. But, in the meantime, if we're to maintain that confidence, we must aim to live lives that are "to the glory and praise of God" (verse 11).

INTRODUCTORY ILLUSTRATION

I was never much good at jigsaw puzzles. When you're staring at this pile of 1000 pieces poured out on the table in front of you, where do you start? Well, apparently what you have to do is find the corner pieces; then you find the pieces with straight edges; then you put them together, so that you have a square frame into which you know everything else fits. You probably still have 874 pieces to fit – but, however confusing it seems, you know they'll all fit into that square. The same is going to be true for the questions that we have as we start **Discipleship Explored**. Even if we have 874 questions we want to ask about God, there are some things that are already in place, as Paul makes clear here in chapter 1: we know that the Lord is sovereign and we know that God is working in us.

OPENING

- Paul wrote this letter to the Christians ("saints in Christ Jesus") who lived at Philippi, which was the main city in Macedonia. This little group of believers were the first Europeans to respond to the good news about Jesus.

- Paul went back to visit them several times after his first visit. But now he writes to them while under house arrest, probably in Rome, and he warns them about some serious dangers that could damage this community of young Christians.

- The theme of Paul's letter to the Philippians is given away in his very first sentence: he describes himself and his colleague Timothy as "servants of Christ" (v1). Like the Philippians reading this letter for the first time 2000 years ago, we're going to be exploring for ourselves exactly what it means to be "servants of Christ". To be, in other words, a disciple.

1. TRUE DISCIPLES HAVE THEIR CONFIDENCE IN GOD

- When someone becomes a Christian, we sometimes say that they have made a decision for Christ, or that someone has committed their life to God. In other words, we think that becoming a Christian is something that we have done.

- Paul sees it differently. The truth is that if you have made a response to God, it is because God has done something in you.

- Paul was certain that God was working in the Philippians because of their "partnership in the gospel from the first day until now" (v5); because their lives have steadily demonstrated that the gospel has changed them. Their words, their actions, even their money (see 4:10, 15–16) had consistently revealed their love for Jesus Christ.

- And because he knew God was working in them, he could also be sure that God would complete the work he started in them (v6).

APPLICATION You may be feeling that since becoming a Christian you keep messing up and sometimes you may even wonder if you really are a Christian. The word "disciple" simply means "learner" – in other words, in the Christian life, we can never say that we have arrived – we will always be learning. Paul's words give us great confidence: he is saying that if God has begun a good work in you, he will finish it.

Add your own illustration here: a personal illustration of how others more readily saw the change in you than you did in yourself. Point out that the Holy Spirit, because he is holy makes us feel bad about the wrong things that we do – but being sensitized to sin, and feeling guilty is a sign that God is at work in us, not that God has abandoned us.

2. TRUE DISCIPLES GROW IN THEIR UNDERSTANDING OF GOD

• Paul tells the Philippian Christians that he is praying that they would (v9) have deeper knowledge and insight.

• One of the effects of this growing knowledge of God (v10) is that "you may be able to discern what is best". In other words, that Christians will be increasingly wise about how to live – and be able to distinguish good from bad.

• But knowledge and understanding are not an end in themselves. God does not want us to become merely experts in theology.

• Knowledge of God is something which gives rise to genuine, intelligent love in a Christian's life: a love for God, for his people and for others.

APPLICATION Are we growing in our knowledge of God, so that we will be able to know what's best in our Christian lives?

3. TRUE DISCIPLES ARE FRUITFUL

• In verse 10, Paul prays that these young Christians would be "pure" and "blameless".

• Paul is saying that a true understanding of God will make us pure through and through.

• But where does this goodness come from? Again, it is not from ourselves. Verse 11 tells us that this "fruit of righteousness" comes from Jesus Christ, and that it brings glory and praise to God.

APPLICATION How "pure" are we? (Are we different on the inside than we are on the outside?) How "blameless" are we? (Do our lives make it easier or harder for other people to believe in Christ?)

CONCLUSION

Growing as a Christian – being a disciple – is something that comes from God, and for which God gets the glory.

Our confidence as Christians comes from the certainty that God always finishes the work he starts. But we are not to just sit around waiting for it to happen to us. The sign that God is at work in us is that we actively take steps to be disciples – to grow in the knowledge of God.

AT THE END OF THE TALK

> *Using Paul's prayer in this passage as a guide, pray for the group.*

> *Introduce the questions in GROUP DISCUSSION 2.*

OUTLINE OF TALK 2
LIVING IN CHRIST
PHILIPPIANS 1:12-26

AIM

• To explain that everything in Paul's life serves one aim – to "advance the gospel". Nothing – not his circumstances, nor his reputation, nor his uncertain future – is allowed to interfere with that aim. In fact, all these things are used by God to fulfill that aim.

INTRODUCTORY ILLUSTRATION

I read this true story recently in a newspaper. A car crashed into Gordon White's living room last week – exactly a year after the same car, driven by the same driver, crashed into the same room. Eric Williams, 60, is believed to have suffered a blackout both times, leaving the road at the same spot in Cleckheaton, West Yorkshire. It took White nine weeks to clear up the mess last time, and a full year to redecorate. "I've only just finished getting the house how I want it," he said. "If I'd known this would happen, I would have used cheaper wallpaper."

If we know what is going to happen in the future, it changes the way we live in the present.

OPENING

• Paul is writing to the Philippians from prison. His circumstances look bad.

• There are people who call themselves Christians, but who are deliberately trying to get him into trouble and ruin his reputation.

• His future looks uncertain as he doesn't know whether he is going to live or die.

• And yet Paul rejoices. Why? Because everything in Paul's life serves one aim – to "advance the gospel" – and nothing is allowed to interfere with that aim.

1. HIS CIRCUMSTANCES ARE BAD, BUT THE GOSPEL IS ADVANCED

- Many people who go through difficult times assume that God has abandoned them.

- Paul sees that God has not abandoned him, but has placed him where he is so that the gospel may be advanced. What seems like a disaster is actually God at work, bringing the good news to others.

- Even though Paul is in prison he makes use of his situation to advance the gospel.

- Not only has Paul been able to talk about Christ to the palace guard (v13), but his example has encouraged others to be more courageous in the way they talk about Jesus (v14).

> *Add your own illustration here: share from your own experience how something that might seem tragic or painful has brought an opportunity to advance the gospel. This is also an opportunity to remind participants what the gospel actually is.*

APPLICATION When somebody in an office, a school staff room, or on a college campus says something about Jesus, it encourages other Christians to say something as well. That was the effect that Paul's imprisonment had on other Christians.

APPLICATION It would have been very easy for Paul to say, "I'll just wait until I get out of prison, then I'll be able to get on with my work for the Lord". But he doesn't do that. No matter what the circumstances, he is looking for opportunities to tell others about Jesus. It's very easy for us to think: "Well, I'll really be able to serve the Lord Jesus better when I've got the job right, when I've got my house sorted out, when my relationships are settled...". We don't wait for our lives to get just right. They never do. God will use you to advance the gospel, whatever circumstances you're in.

2. HIS REPUTATION IS ATTACKED, BUT THE GOSPEL IS ADVANCED

- It's clear from verses 15–18 that Paul's imprisonment has provoked different reactions in the Christian community. Some understand that Paul has been put in prison "for the defence of the gospel" (v16), but others see it as an opportunity to "stir up trouble" for him (v17).

- Verse 18 is important – Paul says: "what does it matter?" The gospel is being preached; Paul's reputation is secondary.

APPLICATION Following Christ may have a negative impact on your reputation. Some people may dismiss you as being "religious" or "holier-than-thou" or "narrow minded" or "weak". Can you say with Paul: "What does it matter?" Is the gospel so important to you that your own reputation is unimportant?

3. HIS FUTURE IS UNCERTAIN, BUT THE GOSPEL IS ADVANCED

- Paul doesn't know whether he is going to live or die.

- Paul hopes that through the Philippians' prayers and with the help of the Spirit (v19) he will have enough courage (v20) to exalt Christ, whether he lives or dies.

- Verse 21 sums up Paul's joyful attitude to life: "To live is Christ" because he will go on preaching Christ if he lives; and "to die is gain", because if he dies he will be with Jesus.

- So whatever happens, Jesus is the object, motive, inspiration and goal of all that Paul does.

APPLICATION As Christians we need not fear death. For us, like Paul, death is "gain": we will be with Christ for eternity in the new heaven and the new earth.

APPLICATION As Christians we need not fear life. Whatever happens to us, God is in control and we should make the most of the time we have to advance the gospel.

CONCLUSION

How would you finish Paul's sentence: "For me to live is …" What? For Paul it is Christ. What is it for us?

AT THE END OF THE TALK

> *Pray for the group.*

> *Introduce the questions in GROUP DISCUSSION 2.*

AIM

• To explain how we can conduct ourselves "in a manner worthy of the gospel" by standing firm together.

INTRODUCTORY ILLUSTRATION

A friend of mine told me this story. He said:

I was walking across a bridge recently. I saw this man who looked like he was ready to jump off. "Don't jump!" I said.

"Why not?" he said. "Nobody loves me."

"God loves you," I said. "You believe in God, don't you?"

"Yes, I believe in God," he said.

"Good," I said. "What religion?"

"Christian," he said.

"Me, too!" I said. "What denomination?"

"Baptist," he said.

"Me, too!" I said. "Independent Baptist or Southern Baptist?"

"Independent Baptist," he said.

"Me, too!" I said. "Moderate Independent Baptist or Conservative Independent Baptist?"

"Conservative Independent Baptist," he said.

"Me, too!" I said. "Calvinistic Conservative Independent Baptist or Arminian Conservative Independent Baptist?"

"Calvinistic Conservative Independent Baptist," he said.

"Me, too!" I said. "Dispensational Premillennial Calvinistic Conservative Independent Baptist or Historical Premillennial Calvinistic Conservative Independent Baptist?"

"Dispensational Premillennial Calvinistic Conservative Independent Baptist," he said.

"Dispensational!" I said, and pushed him off.

Some disagreements can be incredibly petty can't they? By contrast, look at what Paul says in verse 27: "stand firm in one spirit, contending as one man for the faith of the gospel".

OPENING

- "For it has been granted to you on behalf of Christ not only to believe on him, but also to suffer for him..." (v29). If suffering is to be the normal experience of the Christian, how are we to conduct ourselves "in a manner worthy of the gospel", as Paul says we should in verse 27?

- Paul insists that the only way to do it is by standing firm "in one spirit" and "as one man" – in other words, by standing firm together. He calls for unity again in chapter 2 verse 2: "...make my joy complete by being like-minded, having the same love, being one in spirit and purpose".

- Why is it so important to stand together? Because it will enable these young Christians to stand without fear ("without being frightened in any way by those who oppose you") and this in itself will be a powerful sign to their opponents that God is on their side (v28).

- How exactly can we stand together in this way? After all, if we're being honest and realistic about human relationships, we know that it is very difficult to be "one in spirit and purpose" with anyone!

- The secret of standing together is revealed in verse 5: "Your attitude should be the same as Christ Jesus".

- That means: considering others better than ourselves; setting privilege aside and becoming like servants.

1. WE SHOULD CONSIDER OTHERS BETTER THAN OURSELVES (vv3-4)

- We must not think of ourselves more highly than we ought, and we must not think of others as less important.

- We must remember that everyone we meet has great value: they are made in the image of God, and Christ died for them.

- God calls people from every nation to follow him. God's new community is supernatural: unlike human communities, it crosses all boundaries of race, class, income, education and geography.

APPLICATION Do we treat people with the same care Jesus did? Are we guilty of any sort of prejudice against other Christians?

2. WE SHOULD SET PRIVILEGE ASIDE (vv6-7)

- This wonderful poem in v6–11 reminds us of Jesus' Identity as God and man (v6–8), his Mission to die on the cross (v8), and his Call that people follow him as Lord (v10–11).

- Jesus is "in very nature God", and yet he deliberately "made himself nothing". He did not consider it worthwhile to stand up for his "rights", as he could have done.

> *Add your own illustration here about "rights" that might be better laid aside for the sake of Christ and the gospel. (e.g. the right to take a holiday every year, to own certain possessions, to get married.)*

APPLICATION Are we willing to make ourselves nothing so that we can stand together in Christ?

3. WE SHOULD BECOME LIKE SERVANTS (vv7–8)

- Literally, the word in verse 7 means "slave". Jesus made himself like a slave, even to the extent of dying for others.

APPLICATION Are we prepared to serve others, even if it costs us dearly?

CONCLUSION

Paul concludes in verses 9–11 with a stunning image of the whole universe "together in Christ", worshipping the Lord.

If we keep this image of the exalted Christ in mind our attitude will become more like his and we will be better able to stand as one man and in one spirit for the gospel.

AT THE END OF THE TALK

> Pray for the group.

> Introduce the questions in GROUP DISCUSSION 2.

TALK 3

OUTLINE OF TALK 4

TRANSFORMED BY CHRIST
PHILIPPIANS 2:12–30

AIM

- To explore what it means for people to "work out" their salvation and "hold out the word of life".

OPENING

> Remind participants of what they've learned in previous weeks.

- Last week, Paul gave us a striking picture of Christ (2:6–11). And here, in verses 12–30, Paul tells the Philippians that they are to be transformed by that picture of radical self-sacrifice.

- He urges them to do two things: firstly "work out your salvation"; and secondly "hold out the word of life".

- Then he gives us a pen portrait of two men who've done just that.

1. WORK OUT YOUR SALVATION (vv12–13)

- "Continue to work out your salvation with fear and trembling..." (v12). Notice that Paul doesn't say "work for" your salvation. He says "work out your salvation", which means that our salvation should display itself outwardly: it should have a visible, tangible effect on our lives.

- We are able to "work out our salvation" because "it is God who works in [us] to will and to act according to his good purpose" (v13). We work out our salvation because God works in us. He enables us to do the things he calls us to do.

> Give an example of a Christian you know who was empowered by God to "will and to act according to his good purpose".

APPLICATION Are we testing the promise in verse 13 for ourselves by "working out our salvation", even if we don't feel we're able?

APPLICATION Did you notice that Paul says they will need to obey God "not only in [Paul's] presence" but also in his absence (v12). How good are we at obedience when we are away from church, during the week, in the home or workplace?

2. HOLD OUT THE WORD OF LIFE (vv14–18)

* In verse 16, Paul assumes that they will "hold out the word of life" (the Greek literally means "hold forth" or "offer"); they will be sharing the gospel with their lives and their lips.

* The strength of our witness to others depends upon us doing "everything without complaining or arguing", being "blameless and pure" (v14–15). Do we sometimes give people a reason to ignore our witness because our lives are not "blameless"?

> *Give some examples of how this happens. You may want to use this illustration: One person I heard of used to go on business trips with married men who called themselves Christians. And he said that he watched these men going from the brothel on Saturday night to church on Sunday morning. And what he said was: "I did not go to the brothel with them and I didn't go to church with them either."*

* If we do live "blameless and pure" lives, then we will "shine like stars" in what Paul calls "a crooked and depraved generation" (v15).

APPLICATION How much do we really stand out from others who are not "children of God" (v15)? And if we do stand out, is it for the right reasons? Is it because we're holding out the word of life and living "blameless" lives?

3. TWO PEOPLE TRANSFORMED BY CHRIST (vv19–30)

- Paul then gives us a glimpse of two people who've been transformed by Christ in just this way: Timothy and Epaphroditus.

> ▶ *You may want to use this illustration: I hate writing job references for people, especially if they've not been very good employees. You're desperately trying to write the truth without being too hurtful. One of my favourite references for a departing employee was this one: "I am sure he will join your company as he leaves ours: fired with enthusiasm." Or what about this one: "You will be very fortunate if you can get this man to work for you."*

- Timothy and Epaphroditus worked with Paul for some time. Let me read you Paul's job references for them.

> ▶ *Read aloud Paul's description of Timothy (vv19–24).*

- Timothy's interests are the interests "of Jesus Christ" (v21). That means taking "a genuine interest" in the welfare of others (v19), and serving together "in the work of the gospel" (v22).

> ▶ *Read aloud Paul's description of Epaphroditus (vv25–30).*

- How might we speak of a Christian friend who had nearly burned themselves out in their efforts for the gospel? Perhaps we'd say they were naive, careless, or even stupid. How does Paul describe Epaphroditus, a man who "almost died for the work of Christ" (v30)? "Welcome him in the Lord with great joy, and honour men like him..." (v29).

CONCLUSION

When others look at our lives, do they see people like the ones Paul mentions in verse 21, those who look out for their own interests? Or do they see people like Timothy and Epaphroditus, whose self-sacrificial lives have been radically transformed by Christ?

AT THE END OF THE TALK

> *Pray for the group.*

> *Introduce the questions in GROUP DISCUSSION 2.*

OUTLINE OF TALK 5

RIGHTEOUS IN CHRIST
PHILIPPIANS 3:1–9

AIM

- To explain that we relate to God not by religion or "right living", but by the righteousness that Christ gives us as a free gift.

INTRODUCTORY ILLUSTRATION

Everyone at work was very impressed with John Henderson. He was always in the office early. He worked right through his lunch hour and stayed late. He never stopped working throughout the day – always on the phone, or madly typing into his computer. It was a shock then that he was eventually fired. It seems that he had been doing none of the work that the company had allocated to him. He had simply been running his own business from his desk in the office.

OPENING

- How can anyone be good enough for God? Or, as the Bible puts it, how can we be "righteous"?

- For some people, the answer to that question lies in "doing good things", whether it be giving to charity, going to church, treating others in the way they like to be treated themselves, and so on.

- To the people Paul describes in verse 2, the answer lies in the practise of circumcision. They believed that God would only accept them if they had this physical mark of allegiance to him.

- Paul knew that these men would undermine the joy he talks about in verse 1, so he warns the Philippians about them again as "a safeguard". In the original Greek, the phrase "watch out for" (v2) is repeated three times for emphasis.

- In verses 2 and 3, Paul deliberately turns the accusations of these men ("dogs... men who do evil... mutilators of the flesh") back on his accusers:

> The term "dogs" is particularly potent. Considered by the Jews to be unclean animals, the term was sometimes applied to Gentiles and lapsed Jews. In other words, "dogs" are those outside the covenant relationship with God. But, says Paul in verse 2, it is those who insist on circumcision who are the real "dogs".

> "Men who do evil" is literally "evil workers". These men were proud of their good "works". You may be performing works, says Paul with biting irony, but they're evil.

> "Mutilators" refers to circumcision, but rather than using the proper Greek word "peritome", Paul uses the Greek word "katatome", which means "cutting". This is a mutilation of the body which is specifically condemned as a pagan practice in the Old Testament (see Leviticus 21:5 and 1 Kings 18:28). Paul only uses the word "peritome" in verse 3, when he speaks about Christians.

- Paul's words are scathing and clear: these teachers are outside the covenant, are evil and are no better than pagans in their religious practice.

TALK 5

APPLICATION We can be tempted to put our trust in things which will do us no good. It may be our church attendance, the fact that our family has been Christian for generations, or our national heritage. God is interested in none of these things. In fact, quite the reverse. Some of those who are most distant from God are the ones who are most "religious".

> *You may want to use an illustration here, for example: being born in a garage does not make you a car; it was the religious people who opposed and finally killed Jesus; even the devil believes the truth about God – but he remains his enemy.*

2. OUR "GOODNESS" CANNOT MAKE US RIGHTEOUS

- Paul argues his case by setting out his own "reasons to put confidence in the flesh" (v4). His pedigree is impeccable. If anyone had grounds for getting right with God on the basis of his religion it was Paul.

- But he adds another element. "… as for legalistic righteousness, faultless." In other words, if anyone could be justified by doing "good things", Paul was the man.

- Paul says all these religious credentials are "rubbish" (literally, "filthy muck") compared with knowing Jesus and the righteousness that comes through faith in him (vv7–9).

APPLICATION Are we putting our trust in our own goodness? We may be generous, kind and willing to help others, but these things cannot make us righteous. Do you think God would have sent his only Son to die if we could get right with him by doing good things?

3. ONLY JESUS CAN MAKE US RIGHTEOUS

- So, how will we live? There are really only two choices:

  We can go the way of people who "put confidence in the flesh" (v4). We can do what Paul used to do: we can try to summon up a righteousness of our own by being extremely religious, by doing as many good things as we possibly can in the hope that – at the end of the day – God will be impressed by what we've done.

  Or, like Paul, we can refuse to place any confidence in the things we've done. We can realize that we'll never be "righteous" by our own effort. We can gladly accept the righteousness that God freely offers us in Christ, trusting in him to make us righteous.

CONCLUSION

Where are you placing your trust now? If God were to say to you: "Why should I let you into heaven" what would you say?

AT THE END OF THE TALK

> Pray for the group.

> Introduce the questions in GROUP DISCUSSION 2.

TALK 5

OUTLINE OF TALK 6
KNOWING CHRIST
PHILIPPIANS 3:10 – 4:1

AIM

- To explain how we can know Christ.

INTRODUCTORY ILLUSTRATION

It's June 1944, and the American, British, Canadian and French allies have landed on the beaches of Normandy. In the East, Hitler's armies are fighting a losing battle against the Russians, the Luftwaffe has been destroyed, the German army is crumbling – everyone knows that the victory is won, and that it will not be long before the war is over. So do they sit around and do nothing? Not at all. There are still hard months of military campaigning to go.

OPENING

- Last week, we saw that Paul has no confidence in his own religious "goodness". Instead, he wants "the righteousness that comes from God and is by faith" in Jesus Christ. That is the only way that any of us can be accepted by God: because of his goodness, not ours.

- But once we've put our trust in Christ, is that it? Do we just sit back, secure in the knowledge that God accepts us?

- Not according to Paul. His desire is "to know Christ" (v10). The word "know" here doesn't just mean "to be acquainted with"; it means "to become like". We can see that from the way Paul continues: "I want to know Christ and the power of his resurrection and the fellowship of sharing in his sufferings, becoming like him in his death..."

- So how can we "know Christ" in this way? Paul gives us four pointers.

1. TO "KNOW CHRIST" WE MUST REALIZE WE ARE NOT THE FINISHED ARTICLE

- Even Paul, arguably the greatest Christian who ever lived, never claims to be perfect (vv12–13: "Not that I have already obtained all this, or have already been made perfect... I do not consider myself yet to have taken hold of it...").

APPLICATION Beware of any Christian – or any teaching – that says you can be a perfect Christian here and now. We should be satisfied with Christ, but dissatisfied with the imperfection of our Christian life. Paul's dissatisfaction with his own Christian life drives him to know Christ better.

> *Add your own personal illustration here: think of a time when God showed you that you still had a lot to learn.*

2. TO "KNOW CHRIST" WE MUST BE SINGLE-MINDED

- There is "one thing I do", says Paul (v13): he forgets "what is behind" and strains towards "what is ahead".

APPLICATION There are two dangers when we look back at our past: we can either become paralysed by regret because of past experiences; or we can become complacent if we rest on past triumphs. But Paul refuses to allow his past to catch up with him like that. He stays focused on "what is ahead".

3. TO "KNOW CHRIST" WE MUST BE DISCIPLINED

- Paul speaks in very physical, strenuous language, as if he's an athlete training for the Olympics (vv12–14: "I press on... straining towards what is ahead... I press on towards the goal...").

- There's no "let go and let God" mentality with Paul. No "stop trying and start trusting" (though of course, Paul knows it's not all about our effort). He knows that if he wants to know Christ, if he wants to become like him, it will require continuous effort.

TALK 6

Have you found it difficult to set aside the time to do your daily Bible reading? Have other things got in the way of being at church or **Discipleship Explored**? We need to be convinced that knowing Christ is the most important thing, if we are to be strong enough to turn off the TV and open our Bibles.

4. TO "KNOW CHRIST" WE MUST SET OUR HEARTS ON HEAVEN

- Verses 18 and 19, describe those who live as "enemies of the cross of Christ". "Their mind is on earthly things"; in other words, they can't see beyond the here and now, and they only live for the present moment. But, says Paul, "our citizenship is in heaven" (v20).

- To know Christ, we must understand that heaven is our home. We are called "heavenwards" (v14), we belong there (v20), our Saviour will return from there (v20), and he will transform "our lowly bodies" (v21) into glorious bodies that will spend eternity there. Keeping that heavenly perspective, says Paul, is "how you should stand firm in the Lord" (4:1).

> *You may want to use this illustration: Supposing we decided that our country was no longer worth living in, and we became convinced that Peru was the place to be. We receive our Peruvian citizenship, but must wait 6 months before we move there. What will we do in the meantime? We will not spend our time building up our attachment to our old country – extending our home, buying things that we will have to leave behind when we move, forming relationships that have no future. We will spend time getting ready to live in our new country – learning the language, the customs, the national anthem, the history – and we will think about and talk to each other about how marvellous it will be when we move there.*

CONCLUSION

Knowing Christ should change the way we look at everything – our homes, our work, our relationships, what we spend our money on, what we give our time to.

AT THE END OF THE TALK

> *Pray for the group.*

> *Introduce the questions in GROUP DISCUSSION 2.*

TALK 6

OUTLINE OF TALK 7
REJOICING IN CHRIST
PHILIPPIANS 4:2-9

AIM

- To explain that because of Christ it is possible to be joyful, even when circumstances are difficult.

INTRODUCTORY ILLUSTRATION

British holidaymakers love to feel anxious. Among the list of unusual complaints revealed this week by top British tour operators was the following: "No-one told us there'd be fish in the sea. The children were startled." One complainant groused that there were too many Spaniards in Spain, another that there wasn't any air-conditioning outside and a third said this: "It took us nine hours to fly to Jamaica from England. It only took the Americans three hours."

OPENING

- Is it possible to be joyful when circumstances are difficult? Is it possible to rejoice, if, for example, our relationships break down (like Euodia and Syntyche in 4:2) or we face persecution (like the Philippian church in 1:29)? Is it possible to be joyful even if our freedom is taken from us, as is the case with Paul?

- Amazingly, that's exactly what Paul commands in chapter 4 verse 4: "Rejoice in the Lord always. I will say it again: Rejoice!" Humanly speaking, such joy is unrealistic. But that phrase "in the Lord" helps us to understand how this joy is possible even in difficult circumstances.

1. PROBLEMS MUST BE RESOLVED (vv2–3)

- In 4:2–3, we read about two women, Euodia and Syntyche, who have fallen out over some matter. It's not as if they're not Christians – Paul says that their names "are in the book of life". But something has driven a wedge between them, despite the fact that they have worked hard together at Paul's side "in the cause of the gospel".

- Paul pleads with them to "agree with each other in the Lord". His words echo what he has already said in chapter 2 verses 3–5: "... consider others better than yourselves... Your attitude should be the same as that of Christ Jesus..." In other words, this problem will only be resolved, and joy will only be restored, if both women are prepared to adopt the attitude of Jesus: taking the initiative, making themselves humble, serving others – even if such actions come at great personal cost.

APPLICATION If we're "in the Lord", we must take the initiative, swallow our pride and be reconciled to those we've fallen out with. And Christians should help other Christians to reconcile.

2. PERSPECTIVE MUST BE REGAINED (vv4–5)

- In verse 5, Paul puts things into perspective by reminding us that "The Lord is near". The Lord is near because he will return soon, at a time no-one will expect him, and draw life as we know it to a close.

- But the Lord is near in another sense too: his Spirit lives in us, if we're Christian, and his presence reminds us that "our citizenship is in heaven" (3:20). It is that intimacy with the Lord that enables our "gentleness [to] be evident to all" (v5) and, again, to "rejoice" (v4).

APPLICATION Because we know that the Lord will return, we must be gentle with everyone. The presence of his Holy Spirit in us will help us to do that.

TALK 7

3. ANXIETY MUST BE REMOVED (vv6–7)

- The antidote to anxiety, says Paul, is prayer. "Do not be anxious about anything", he says, "but in everything, by prayer and petition, with thanksgiving, present your requests to God" (v6).

- Our anxiety is removed because as we pray we are reminded of all the blessings we have in Christ, not least the fact that we are able to pray to God!

- As we offer our requests and our thanks, "the peace of God, which transcends all understanding, will guard your hearts and your minds in Christ Jesus" (v7).

- It's an amazing promise: not that God will take away difficult circumstances, but that "the peace of God", protects us from anxiety and worry even in difficult circumstances.

APPLICATION If we often feel anxious and imagine that God is far from us, is it because we are spending so little time with him in grateful prayer?

4. OUR MINDS MUST BE PURE (vv8–9)

- Paul leaves us with a challenge in verses 8–9, a challenge to the way we use our minds. After all, we know that what we put into our bodies has a big impact on our physical health. How careful are we about what we put into our minds?

- Paul says in verses 8–9 that we must set our minds on things that are true, noble, right, pure, lovely, admirable, excellent and praiseworthy. That in itself will have a huge impact on our ability to rejoice in difficult circumstances (because if we put these things into practice, "the God of peace will be with you" – verse 9).

APPLICATION How accurately does verse 8 describe the things we put into our minds?

CONCLUSION

Rejoicing in Christ is not something that comes naturally – we have to work at it!

AT THE END OF THE TALK

> Pray for the group.

> Introduce the questions in GROUP DISCUSSION 2.

AIM

- To explain that contentment and generosity are marks of a true disciple.

INTRODUCTORY ILLUSTRATION

I saw this article in *The Independent on Sunday* and it's called "The Experts' Guide to a Happy Life". Various people tell you how you can be content. Diane, a beautician from Cardiff says "One thing I'd like to say to make people happy is that women are all hairier than you think. You are not alone." Nicholas, a lawyer from London, says, "If you're looking to live a smooth, sorted financial life, then you've got to open your post. The type of person who is going to go bankrupt will be very good at denial. They're often charming people who are used to getting away with things. If you want to be happy, don't marry one of these people." Vic, a concierge from London, says, "Never do anything embarrassing in a lift."

OPENING

- "I have learned to be content whatever the circumstances," says Paul in chapter 4 verse 11. Are we able to say the same thing?

- The word "content" in Philippians 4 literally means "complete". So Paul is saying that he doesn't get his sense of completeness from the things he owns, the food he eats, the job he does, the place he lives or the friends he has.

- He says it again in verse 12: "I have learned the secret of being content in any and every situation...". In this final passage of Philippians, Paul reveals the secret of contentment.

1. WE CAN BE CONFIDENT IN GOD'S POWER

• "I can do everything through him who gives me strength", says Paul in verse 13.

• The whole of Paul's letter sings with this confidence in God's power: "he who began a good work in you will carry it on to completion" (1:6); "I am confident in the Lord..." (2:24); "...if on some point you think differently, that too God will make clear to you" (3:15); "...[the Lord Jesus] will transform our lowly bodies so that they will be like his glorious body" (3:21); "... the peace of God... will guard your hearts and your minds in Christ Jesus" (4:7); and so on.

APPLICATION We must have that confidence too, if we're to be content in every situation.

> *Put a personal illustration here, perhaps about a time when you placed too much confidence in yourself, and failed.*

2. WE CAN BE CONFIDENT IN GOD'S PROVISION

• As we saw in chapter 3, Paul encourages us to be discontented with our knowledge and experience of God (3:12). Here, on the other hand, he implies that we should be thoroughly content with whatever God – in his loving wisdom – gives us.

• Whether we are wealthy or lack material things; whether we are healthy or face debilitating illness; whether we are single or married; whether we live in a free country, or suffer in chains like Paul – we must remain confident of one thing: God will meet all our needs "according to his glorious riches in Christ Jesus" (v9).

APPLICATION This is not a guarantee that God will make us healthy, wealthy and popular, but it is a guarantee that he will meet all our needs.

> *Illustrate this with a testimony from your own life, or from someone known to you.*

• Paul demonstrates this confidence in his attitude to the gifts the Philippians have sent him.

TALK 8

- He is delighted that the Philippians have sent him a gift (v10), and he is extremely grateful for the repeated and self-sacrificial giving that has characterized their Christian lives (vv15–16). He describes what they've done as "a fragrant offering, an acceptable sacrifice, pleasing to God" (v18).

- But even so, Paul doesn't depend upon their gifts to make him content. Far from it! As he says himself in verse 11, "I am not saying this because I am in need, for I have learned to be content whatever the circumstances". He is content because he knows that – whatever happens – God will meet all his needs.

APPLICATION   We need that confidence too, if we're to be content. We need to be confident in God's power, and confident in God's provision. That's the example Paul sets.

CONCLUSION

Here we are at the end of this letter and the end of *Discipleship Explored*. Paul has taught us many things: to remember that God always finishes the work he starts; to contend for the gospel; to look to the interests of others; to show our salvation in the way we live; to remember that only Christ can make us righteous; to set our hearts on heaven; to rejoice in the Lord; to be content in all circumstances. And to do all these things for the glory of God (v20).

And did you notice what Paul wrote in verse 22? He says "all the saints send you greetings, especially those who belong to Caesar's household." Even though Paul has been taken captive in the Roman Empire at Caesar's pleasure, he reminds us that even Caesar's household has been taken captive by the glorious gospel of Jesus Christ.

AT THE END OF THE TALK

> *Pray for the group.*

> *Introduce the questions in GROUP DISCUSSION 2.*

SETTING UP THE COURSE
GETTING FEEDBACK

Feedback forms, given out during the last week of the course, are a great way to challenge participants to think about what they have learned, and to help leaders plan a way forward once the course is ended. An example feedback form is given below. (You can also download the form from www.discipleshipexplored.org)

We are always seeking to improve *Discipleship Explored* and would value your feedback.

Your details (optional):

Name _____ Date _____

Address _____

Telephone _____ Email _____

1 Why did you come to *Discipleship Explored*?

2 On a scale of 1–5 (1 being poor and 5 excellent) how would you rate:

   Group Discussions ☐

   Talks ☐

   THE WEEK AHEAD studies ☐

   Food ☐

   Overall ☐

3 What did you enjoy most about the course?

4 What can we improve?

5 What would you like to do now?

   ☐ I would like to join a Bible study group

   ☐ I would like to discuss things further with someone

   ☐ Other _____

This section is intended for every leader, and will prepare you to lead participants through the course.

- Read through this section, completing the exercises as you go.

- Before the course begins, set aside a few hours when you and your co-leaders can meet for a meal, to pray together, get to know one another and discuss any practical issues that may have arisen from reading this section.

TRAINING NOTES

TRAINING NOTES
INTRODUCING DISCIPLESHIP EXPLORED

Are you content in every situation? Are you sure of your salvation? Are you able to say with conviction: "to me, to live is Christ and to die is gain"?

The book of Philippians is full of challenge and reassurance – particularly for those who, like the Philippians themselves, are just beginning the Christian life. **Discipleship Explored** is an eight-week exploration of what it means to be a wholehearted disciple of Jesus Christ.

If you are familiar with **Christianity Explored**, you'll feel right at home. Each week consists of a meal, a Bible study, a short talk and a group discussion. In addition, THE WEEK AHEAD studies give you and participants a Bible reading plan for the week.

	Group Discussion 1	Talk	Group Discussion 2	The Week Ahead
WEEK 1	Welcome	Phil 1:1–11 Confident in Christ	Discuss Talk	Assurance
WEEK 2	Bible Study Phil 1:9–11	Phil 1:12–26 Living in Christ	Discuss Talk	The Holy Spirit
WEEK 3	Bible Study Phil 1:21–26	Phil 1:27 – 2:11 Standing Together in Christ	Discuss Talk	The Cross
WEEK 4	Bible Study Phil 2:5–11	Phil 2:12–30 Transformed by Christ	Discuss Talk	Salvation
WEEK 5	Bible Study Phil 2:19–30	Phil 3:1–9 Righteous in Christ	Discuss Talk	Righteousness
WEEK 6	Bible Study Phil 3:1–4	Phil 3:10 – 4:1 Knowing Christ	Discuss Talk	Trusting God
WEEK 7	Bible Study Phil 3:10–11	Phil 4:2–9 Rejoicing in Christ	Discuss Talk	Prayer
WEEK 8	Bible Study Phil 4:8–9	Phil 4:10–23 Content in Christ	Discuss Talk	Contentment

We are called to be disciples and make disciples. Jesus commanded Christians to "go and make disciples of all nations, baptizing them in the name of the Father and of the Son and of the Holy Spirit, and teaching them to obey everything I have commanded you." (Matthew 28:19–20).

People learn about what it means to be a disciple, not just from the things we teach, but from our behaviour as well. That's why Paul tells Timothy to "set an example for the believers in speech, in life, in love, in faith and in purity... watch your life and doctrine closely" (1 Timothy 4:12, 16).

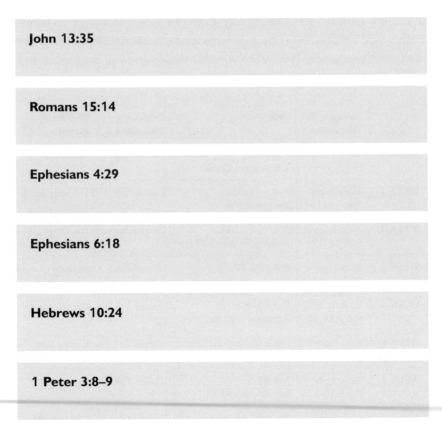

> *Read the following verses and then write down what it will mean for you to "set an example" during* **Discipleship Explored**.

John 13:35

Romans 15:14

Ephesians 4:29

Ephesians 6:18

Hebrews 10:24

1 Peter 3:8–9

> *Pray that you would be able to put these verses into practice.*

TRAINING NOTES
BEFORE THE COURSE

Before the course starts there are a number of things you should do:

GET TO KNOW THE STUDY GUIDE

Read Philippians at least three times and familiarize yourself with the *Study Guide* part of this book.

You will feel much more confident to lead participants once you've prepared yourself for the Bible studies and discussions that make up the course.

GET TO KNOW YOUR FELLOW LEADERS

You will be praying, studying and teaching participants together, so it's important to get to know each other before you begin. (See 1 Corinthians 12:25)

It is also good to reach agreement on how you would handle some of the pastoral issues outlined on the next page.

PRAY

- that those invited will attend the course

- that God would help them learn to stand firm in their faith

- for the logistics of organizing the course

- for good relationships with co-leaders and with participants

- that God would equip you to lead faithfully

- that the Holy Spirit would commend God's word to hearts and minds

ANTICIPATE PASTORAL ISSUES

Try to anticipate the pastoral issues that are likely to arise for young Christians. Think about how you would help people with these issues and which parts of the Bible will be particularly relevant to them.

How would you help a person who was...

... **sleeping with a partner**

... **dealing with addictions**

... **unsure that God can forgive them for something they've done**

... **coping with broken family relationships**

... **dating a non-Christian girlfriend or boyfriend**

... **worried that they are not a Christian**

... **rejected by non-Christian friends or family**

TRAINING NOTES
DURING THE COURSE

A typical week on *Discipleship Explored* looks like this:

Leaders' prayer meeting	15 minutes
Sharing a meal	25 minutes
Group Discussion 1	30 minutes
Talk	20 minutes
Group Discussion 2	30 minutes

LEADERS' PRAYER MEETING

Arrive in plenty of time so that you can pray with the other leaders. Pray for individual participants, that God will help them grasp the truths that will be presented that week. Pray too for the person delivering the talk and for one another.

It may be helpful each week to use one of Paul's prayers as a model for your own. Try praying through:

1 Thessalonians 5:23–24	(Week 1)
Ephesians 1:17–19	(Week 2)
2 Thessalonians 1:11–12	(Week 3)
Philemon 4–6	(Week 4)
2 Thessalonians 2:16–17	(Week 5)
Ephesians 3:16–19	(Week 6)
1 Thessalonians 3:12–13	(Week 7)
Colossians 1:9–12	(Week 8)

SHARING A MEAL

Eating together is an important part of each week as it helps people to feel comfortable in the group.

Of course, the meal is also a great opportunity to model the importance of giving thanks to God. One of the leaders should be ready to give thanks each week for the food that has been prepared.

GROUP DISCUSSION 1

This discussion has two components.

First, groups discuss any questions participants may have from THE WEEK AHEAD. (These are studies that participants have completed at home during the previous week.)

Second, groups look together at a passage from Philippians. (Typically, this will be a few verses from the passage looked at in the previous week.)

▶ See page 9 for an example of this.

As a leader, your responsibility is more than just asking the Bible study questions. You should try to maintain a relaxed atmosphere and involve everyone in the discussion. Don't forget how important the tone of your voice and your body language can be as you lead the discussion.

It is important to listen carefully to the answers given by participants and to reply graciously. Participants need to know that they are valued and that their opinions are important to you.

Remember that this is a group of new Christians so they may not know the Bible well. Give page numbers when turning to passages and, if possible, give some brief background information on the relevant book. e.g. "This passage is from 1 Peter, a letter that Peter wrote to Christians who were being persecuted. Peter, as you'll remember, was one of Jesus' disciples."

Be aware that some words and phrases will be unfamiliar to new Christians so be ready to explain them. (e.g. "saints"; "righteousness"; "drink offering")

Encourage participants to write down the answers in the space provided in their *Study Guide*. The answers are provided for you.

You should be able to complete GROUP DISCUSSION 1 in 30 minutes, but if you are behind schedule, don't feel that you have to complete all the questions. If participants are stuck on some aspect of the Bible study, either from Philippians or from their readings at home, take time to explore things further.

TALK

After GROUP DISCUSSION 1, a talk is presented.

Each week, just before the talk, one of the leaders will be asked to read the relevant passage from Philippians out loud.

GROUP DISCUSSION 2

Use the questions to help your group explore the truths that have been presented.

> See page 11 for an example of this.

It is not important to finish all the questions. They are just a guide to discussion. Add your own supplementary questions as necessary to ensure that participants have understood the passage from Philippians.

Many questions in this section have personal applications. Depending on your group, participants may feel shy about answering these in front of others. Giving your own answer may encourage them to do so. Otherwise, feel free to ask participants to answer the questions privately at home.

Philippians will provoke and challenge even the most mature Christians so it will be appropriate to pray at the end of the study. There are a number of different ways you might approach this, depending on how confident your group are.

- You might choose simply to pray on behalf of the whole group about the issues that have been raised in Philippians.

- Alternatively, you might ask each of the participants in turn what they would like prayer for, and then pray on behalf of the whole group.

- For groups who are able, encourage praying aloud for one another. Hopefully, by the end of the course all groups should be willing to pray in this way.

Encourage participants to use THE WEEK AHEAD studies as their daily readings for the coming week. (These studies are designed to help participants establish a pattern of daily Bible reading and prayer.) Explain that you'll also be doing the studies and that there will be time to discuss them next week. You may want to introduce briefly what the studies will be about as a way of encouraging them to do it.

Go through THE WEEK AHEAD Bible studies as your own daily readings. If you fill in the answers yourself you will be much better able to help the participants understand the passages assigned.

Always finish at the promised time. Good timekeeping develops trust in the group, and people will be more likely to return next week. However, let participants know that they are welcome to stay and talk further if they like. As the course progresses, many participants will need your advice and support as they seek to serve Christ wholeheartedly.

TRAINING NOTES
WHAT DO I DO IF...

... THERE'S SILENCE?

If a question is met with silence, don't be too quick to speak. Allow people time to think. They might be considering how to phrase their answer.

If you sense that someone knows the answer but is shy about giving it, ask them by name. Often they will be happy to be asked.

It might be appropriate to try a "game" – asking them to raise their hand if they agree or disagree with certain answers as you give them.

It may help to divide people into groups of two or three to work through questions and then have them feed their answers back to the whole group.

... ONE PERSON ANSWERS ALL THE QUESTIONS?

Thank them for their answers. Try asking the group, "What do other people think?"

Direct a few questions at the other participants by name.

Sit beside the talkative participant the following week. That will make it harder for them to catch your eye and answer the questions.

If the situation continues, you may need to say something to the participant after the study and ask them to give others an opportunity to answer next time. (For example, "Thank you so much for everything you are contributing. I wonder if you could help me with the quieter people in the group ...")

... SOMEONE GIVES THE WRONG ANSWER?

Do not immediately correct them. Give the person the opportunity to correct themselves. Ask them, for example, "What does verse 4 tell us about that?" If they are still unable to answer correctly, give others the chance (for example, "Does anyone disagree or want to add anything?").

If necessary, don't be afraid graciously to correct a wrong answer that may mislead others. Say something like, "Thank you, that's an interesting point, but I'm not sure that's what's going on here."

Have further questions in mind to develop the initial answer, for example, "What did you mean by that?" or "What does everyone else think?" or "Where does it say that?"

If no-one is able to answer the question, give the correct answer, showing from the Bible passage why it is the right answer.

... SOMEONE ASKS A QUESTION I CANNOT ANSWER?

Lead honestly. You won't be able to answer every question. Some questions can be easily addressed, but others will be difficult.

If you don't know the answer, say so – but tell them that you'll try to have an answer ready for the following week.

It may be best to give them a suitable book to help them. See www.discipleshipexplored.org/reading for suggestions.

... PARTICIPANTS DON'T COME BACK?

If you've already established a good relationship with that person, contact him or her once to say you missed them and that it would be great to see them next week, but don't put pressure on them.

... PARTICIPANTS MISS A WEEK OR MORE?

Welcome them back and during the meal try and summarize what they have missed. Encourage them to read the passages in Philippians they have missed and to work through the questions in GROUP DISCUSSION 2 as their daily reading. Let them know that they can come back to you with anything they are concerned about or do not understand.

... IT BECOMES APPARENT THAT A PARTICIPANT IS NOT A CHRISTIAN?

If they have not already attended **Christianity Explored**, explain that it may be more useful as an introduction for them and escort them to the next course. If the next course does not start for some time, consider meeting with them on an individual basis and taking them through **Christianity Explored**.

If they have already been through **Christianity Explored**, then don't worry. As long as they aren't keeping the group from learning, let them carry on attending. They are hearing God's word, and that will do its work (Isaiah 55:10–11).

If they are preventing the group from learning, it may be appropriate to pull them out of the group and meet on a one-to-one basis to study a Gospel together.

... PARTICIPANTS DON'T SEEM TO BE "GROWING"?

Remember that no matter how much biblical knowledge we share, or how exemplary our lives are, only God can enable our participants to mature as Christians. We need to allow God to work in his time and in his way ("I planted the seed and Apollos watered it, but God made it grow" 1 Corinthians 3:6).

However we can – and must – pray that God would make them grow.

...THE PASTORAL ISSUE THEY CONFIDE IN ME IS ONE I AM NOT QUALIFIED TO DEAL WITH?

It is best not to try and deal with situations if you feel you are out of your depth. Encourage the person to go with you to see your pastor or a Christian counsellor.

Pray with them about the issue.

Do not break their confidence without asking their permission first. However, in extreme circumstances you may need to do so even if they refuse to give you permission.

TRAINING NOTES
INTRODUCING PHILIPPIANS

WHO WROTE IT?

The apostle Paul wrote the letter to the Philippians.

Not only is Paul's writing style much in evidence, but the early church unanimously declared it to be his work.

WHERE WAS IT WRITTEN?

Philippians 1:13–14 tells us that Paul wrote the letter while in prison, most likely when he was under house arrest in Rome.

Acts 28:14–31 reveals some fascinating details about this period of Paul's life: he was allowed to live by himself in his own rented house, albeit with a soldier to guard him. He was also free to receive visitors, preaching and teaching "boldly and without hindrance".

WHEN WAS IT WRITTEN?

The evidence suggests that it was written around AD 61.

WHO WAS HE WRITING TO?

The city of Philippi in Greece was a successful Roman colony whose inhabitants prided themselves on being Roman citizens.

Many Philippians made a point of speaking Latin, and even dressed like Romans.

WHY WAS IT WRITTEN?

Paul wanted to thank the Philippian Christians for the gift they had sent him, when they found out he had been detained in Rome.

But he does several other things too: he reports on his present circumstances; he encourages them to stand firm and rejoice in the face of persecution; he urges them to be humble and united; and he warns them against certain dangerous people within their church (see Philippians 3).

WHAT IS DISTINCTIVE ABOUT THE LETTER?

Philippians is a radical picture of what it means to be a Christian: self-humbling (2:1–4), single-minded (3:13–14), anxiety-free (4:6), and able to do all things (4:13).

Unusually, Philippians contains no Old Testament quotations, perhaps because there was no synagogue in Philippi.

It is also the New Testament letter of joy: the word, in its various forms, occurs 16 times in Philippians.

> *In order to further familiarize yourself with Philippians you should read the talk outlines on pages viii to xxxviii.*

TRAINING NOTES
AFTER THE COURSE

It is vital to have follow-up in place:

STAY IN TOUCH

Plan to stay in touch with all the members of your group, and arrange it with your co-leaders so that each participant has at least one person who remains in touch with him or her.

ARRANGE FOLLOW-UP

Encourage them to join a Bible study group in their church and to find something they can do to help the work of their church and to serve others.

PRAY

Pray especially that they would be able to put into practice what they have learned from Philippians.

This section contains the studies to work through over the eight-week course. It is an exact duplicate of the material in the participant's *Study Guide*. However it also contains specific instructions for leaders, additional notes and the answers to the questions in GROUP DISCUSSION 1.

- The page numbers in this section are the same as those in the participant's *Study Guide* for easy reference.

- If participants miss a week, take time during the meal to summarize briefly what was taught the week before.

- At the end of GROUP DISCUSSION 2 don't forget to pray with your group and encourage them to complete THE WEEK AHEAD studies.

- Go through THE WEEK AHEAD studies as your daily readings. If you fill in the answers yourself you will be much better able to help the participants understand the passages assigned.

SECTION 3

STUDY GUIDE

WEEK 1
CONFIDENT IN CHRIST

GROUP DISCUSSION 1

> Welcome the participants, introduce yourself to the group and ask them to do the same.

> Please give each participant a Bible and a copy of the Study Guide. Briefly explain the format of each week.

> Ask participants to turn to Week 1 on page 3 of their Study Guide.

> Use the time to get to know one another.

TALK   PHILIPPIANS 1:1–11

Additional notes for leaders:

Saints (v1) – "holy ones"; "set apart ones"; in other words, God's people. Saints are not just a few special people, but all Christians.

The day of Christ (v6, v10) – when Jesus returns.

1 Was there anything in the talk you didn't understand, you disagree with or that you found particularly interesting?

2 According to verse 6, what confidence should we have as Christians?

3 In the midst of daily life, why is verse 6 sometimes hard to believe?

4 What can we hold on to when we lack confidence in our salvation?

5 What difference should this confidence make to our lives?

6 What is the result of God's "good work in you" and when will it be complete? (see verses 6, 10, 11)

THE WEEK AHEAD

Each week, THE WEEK AHEAD gives participants a plan to help them read the Bible every day. Use the studies as your own daily readings so that you are able to help participants with any questions they may have when you next meet. The studies this week help to explain how we can be confident of our salvation.

SUNDAY

> Read the passage that will be preached at the church service you attend.

On the other six days...

DAY 1

> Re-read Philippians 1:1–11 and think about the answers you gave to the questions in GROUP DISCUSSION 2 on the opposite page.

> Thank God that he will complete the "good work" that he began in you.

DAY 2

> Read 1 John 1:5 – 2:1.

John wrote this letter in around 90AD and it is probably a circular letter intended for a number of churches.

1 What is "walking in the light"? (see verses 6 and 7)

(Clue: Walking in the light apparently needs the purification of the blood of Jesus, so it can't mean "being perfect". Remember the chief characteristic of light is to reveal things. Take a look at John 3:20–21.)

continued »

2 So, what is "walking in the darkness"? (see verses 5 and 6)

3 Put verse 8 into your own words.

4 How can we be certain that confessing sin will result in our forgiveness? (see verse 9)

5 What is encouraging about the balance of chapter 2 verse 1?

> *Spend a few minutes thanking God for the secure faith you have, which is based upon what Jesus has already done for you.*

DAY 3

> *Read John 6:35–40.*

These verses are taken from a discussion the crowd are having with Jesus after the feeding of the 5,000. The crowd demand a miraculous sign like the one Moses gave when he fed the people of Israel with manna in the wilderness.

Jesus reminds them that it was his Father in heaven who fed the people. And in any case, says Jesus, the "true bread" is "he who comes down from heaven and gives life to the world."

continued »

1 What "life" does Jesus bring? (see verse 35)

(Clue: Look at what John 3:16 says about the reason Jesus was sent.)

2 Look at the promise in verse 37. How can you be sure that you are included in this promise?

3 God's plan for us is clearly given in verses 39 and 40. What is God's part in this plan?

4 What is our part?

Use these verses to thank God for what he is doing in your life and to pray about the coming weeks at **Discipleship Explored**.

DAY 4

Read Ephesians 2:8–10.

Paul wrote this letter to the church in Ephesus. These verses explain very clearly how we have been saved.

continued

1 According to verses 8 and 9, what is it that saves us?

2 What is it that Paul says has no power to save us?

(Note: He mentions these because it is all too easy to rely on them rather than God.)

3 Put verse 8 into your own words.

4 Verse 10 is packed with meaning. What are the three things we learn? All three are God-centred and God-initiated.

> *Pray that God would enable you to rely solely on him.*

DAY 5

> *Re-read the Bible passages you've read over the past week. Choose a verse that you found particularly helpful, write it down in the space below and memorize it.*

DAY 6

> *Read Philippians 1:12–26 in preparation for* **Discipleship Explored**.

WEEK 2
LIVING IN CHRIST

GROUP DISCUSSION 1

> *Ask participants to turn to Week 2 on page 9 of their Study Guide.*

> *Ask if anyone has any questions arising from last week's studies and discuss as necessary.*

> *Ask participants to turn to Philippians 1:9–11. A leader – or one of the participants – should read the passage aloud and the group should then work through the study below. The answers are printed here for your reference.*

1 What does Paul pray for the Philippian Christians?

That their love for God and other people may grow.

That this love will be shaped by knowledge and depth of insight.

2 Why does he pray for these things? (see verse 10)

So that they would know how to live in a way that honours God.

Note: There is a logical sequence here. As our love grows, we are able to "discern what is best", and thus be "pure and blameless".

3 What does Paul hope will be the result of this? (see verse 11)

That they would be full of the fruit of righteousness, pleasing to God in every way, so that God gets the glory and praise.

4 How might Paul's prayer shape the way we pray for other Christians?

Suggest that participants use these verses as a basis for their prayers for themselves and for other Christians during the coming week.

Additional notes for leaders:

Preach Christ (v15) – explain all that Christ has done for us at the cross; tell the gospel.

Deliverance (v19) – cannot mean deliverance from prison, because that would make the sentence contradictory: how could "what has happened to me" (i.e. prison) "turn out for my deliverance" (i.e. release from prison). The word translated "deliverance" is "soteria", which is usually translated "salvation".

1 Was there anything in the talk you didn't understand, you disagree with or that you found particularly interesting?

2 Paul's greatest ambition was for the gospel to spread. What is your greatest ambition? (Be honest!)

3 What pressures did Paul face that may have led him to put his own desires first? (see verses 13, 15–17, 23)

4 What was his attitude to these pressures and why?

5 How might our circumstances, reputation or future plans affect our desire to tell others about Christ?

6 How would you put Paul's motto in verse 21, "To live is Christ and to die is gain", into your own words?

7 How would your friends or colleagues finish this sentence: "For me to live is…"?

8 What about you? How would you finish that same sentence?

THE WEEK AHEAD

In Philippians 1:19, Paul tells the Philippian church that he has been helped by their prayers and "the Spirit of Jesus Christ". The studies this week will tell us more about the Holy Spirit and what he does.

SUNDAY

> Read the passage that will be preached at the church service you attend.

On the other six days...

DAY 1

> Re-read Philippians 1:12–26 and think about the answers you gave to the questions in GROUP DISCUSSION 2 on the previous page.

> Pray that you would be able to echo Paul's motto with conviction: "for to me, to live is Christ and to die is gain".

DAY 2

> Read John 14:15–31.

In this passage, Jesus is speaking just hours before his death. He wants the disciples to know that they won't be alone when he leaves them. The Holy Spirit will be given to them, and will be with them forever.

The word translated "Counsellor" in this passage is literally "one who comes alongside"; an advocate. The word "another" is very significant here. Jesus is the first "one who comes alongside" and the Holy Spirit will follow him, so the Holy Spirit is a person. Notice too that in verse 17 the Holy Spirit is referred to as "him" and "he".

continued »

1 How does Jesus describe the Holy Spirit in verse 16?

WEEK 2

2 In verses 17 and 18, what is the difference between the world's relationship to the Holy Spirit and ours?

(Note: Jesus describes the relationship between himself, the Father and the Holy Spirit as very close indeed. Jesus says in verse 17 that the Holy Spirit is in us and he also says in verse 20 that he – Jesus – is in us.)

3 The main theme in this passage is love (verses 15, 21, 23, 24). How is our love for Jesus shown in practice? (see verses 21 and 23)

4 What is the consequence of living in this way?

> *Thank God for the work of the Holy Spirit in your life, asking that he would increase your understanding of the Bible. Pray that you would increasingly demonstrate your love for Jesus by obedience (verse 15).*

> *Read John 16:5–15.*

1 What are the three ways in which the Holy Spirit convicts the world? (see verse 8)

2 How does Jesus explain these three in verses 9 to 11?

3 Jesus promises the apostles in verse 13 that the Holy Spirit will guide them into "all truth". How does this promise give us confidence as we read the New Testament?

It is very important to see that the Holy Spirit's role is to draw attention to Jesus.

> *Read verses 14 and 15 again, and also John 15:26. Ask the Holy Spirit to make Jesus more real to you as you read the Bible.*

DAY 4

> *Read Acts 2:1–13.*

Acts was written by the same Luke who wrote the Gospel. In fact, as you can see from the start of both books, both were originally intended for the same reader, Theophilus.

Acts 2:1–13 records the way in which the Holy Spirit was given to the church on the day of Pentecost. (The day of Pentecost was the fiftieth day after the Sabbath of Passover week, hence the Greek name meaning "fifty". It was a celebration of the end of the barley harvest and a feast of the "first fruits" of the harvest.)

1 What was the effect of the disciples being filled with the Holy Spirit? (verse 4; see also verse 6)

2 What was it the disciples were saying to the people as they did this? (see verse 11)

3 Read Genesis 11:1–9. How does this contrast with what happened on the day of Pentecost?

continued >>

In the Old Testament, the Holy Spirit was only given to people with particular roles – prophets, kings and priests. But Acts 2:17–18 quotes a prophecy from the prophet Joel that, one day, the Holy Spirit would fill every one of God's people, in every nation. The day of Pentecost was the fulfillment of that prophecy.

> *Spend time praying, thanking God for the Holy Spirit's presence in your life.*

DAY 5

> *Re-read the Bible passages you've read over the past week. Choose a verse that you found particularly helpful, write it down in the space below and memorize it.*

DAY 6

> *Read Philippians 1:27 – 2:11 in preparation for* **Discipleship Explored**.

WEEK 3
STANDING TOGETHER IN CHRIST

GROUP DISCUSSION 1

> Ask participants to turn to Week 3 on page 17 of their Study Guide.

> Ask if anyone has any questions arising from last week's studies and discuss as necessary.

> Ask participants to turn to Philippians 1:21–26. A leader – or one of the participants – should read the passage aloud and the group should then work through the study below. The answers are printed here for your reference.

1 What dilemma does Paul face?

He is torn between wanting to live or die.

2 Why does Paul want to "go on living"?

It would be a benefit to the Philippians. By being with them again he would help them to progress in their faith and find joy in Christ.

Note: This is what Paul means by "fruitful labour" in verse 22.

3 What is it about death that Paul finds so attractive? (see verse 23)

He would then "be with Christ, which is better by far".

4 Do you share Paul's view of death? Why or why not?

It may be useful to look at 2 Corinthians 5:1–8 and Revelation 21:1–7.

5 What do these verses tell us about Paul's mindset?

For Paul, Christ is central to everything.

Additional notes for leaders:

Worthy of the gospel (v27) – this does not imply we can make ourselves worthy to receive the gospel and salvation, but means that having been forgiven by God, we should live lives that are consistent with being his people.

Granted to you... to suffer for him (v29) – granted means given as a privilege. So Christian suffering, as well as faith, is a privilege. Note that the suffering Paul speaks of is explicitly Christian: it is the result of "contending... for the faith of the gospel". (see also Matthew 5:11–12; Acts 5:41; 1 Peter 4:14)

Fellowship in the Spirit (v1) – all believers have received the Holy Spirit and are therefore linked to one another.

Every knee should bow (v10) – this cannot mean that everyone will one day come to faith. Isaiah 45:22–24 makes clear that although all will bow, those who are rebellious will still "be put to shame" at judgement.

1 Was there anything in the talk you didn't understand, you disagree with or that you found particularly interesting?

2 According to Philippians 1:27, what does it mean to conduct ourselves "in a manner worthy of the gospel of Christ"?

3 What opportunities do you have to "contend" for the gospel by sharing your faith with others?

4 Paul and the Philippian church faced opposition because they were "contending" for the gospel (see verses 28–30). Why might we face opposition to the gospel today?

5 In verses 28–30 Paul makes some surprising statements. From these verses, what should we remember when we face opposition?

6 What does it mean to stand together, according to Paul in Philippians 2:2?

7 What will it mean in practice for us to "consider others better" than ourselves?

THE WEEK AHEAD

Philippians 2:5–11 are a wonderful insight into the humility and selflessness of Jesus. The studies this week focus on Jesus and his mission to rescue us from our sin.

SUNDAY

> Read the passage that will be preached at the church service you attend.

On the other six days...

DAY 1

> Re-read Philippians 1:27 – 2:11 and think about the answers you gave to the questions in GROUP DISCUSSION 2 on the previous page.

> Pray for strength and wisdom so that wherever you are your attitude is "the same as that of Christ Jesus".

DAY 2

> Read Isaiah 53:1–12.

These verses, describing the suffering of God's "servant", were written about 700 years before Jesus was born. It is remarkable that so much of Jesus' mission is prophesied here.

1 Looking at verses 4–6, what similarities can you find between the "servant" and Jesus Christ?

(Note: "transgressions" and "iniquities" are another way of describing "sin".)

continued

2 What does the servant's suffering achieve?

3 Why is this suffering necessary? (see verse 6)

4 In Acts 8:26–35, the Ethiopian is reading verses 7–8 of Isaiah 53. How do you think Philip used these verses to tell the Ethiopian "the good news about Jesus" (Acts 8:35)?

5 Read 1 Peter 2:22–25. Which verses from Isaiah 53 can you detect in this passage?

> *Give thanks to God for the good news of Jesus.*

> *Read Luke 15:1–32.*

Notice the context of these parables in verses 1 and 2. The comment in verse 2 was meant as an insult, but for us it is very good news.

1 What do the three parables tell us about the mission of Jesus and how God views "sinners"?

2 The Parable of the Lost Son has a bit more detail in it than the other two. Verse 20 is a very bold picture of God. What might surprise non-Christians about this verse?

3 Jesus probably intended the Pharisees (who were listening, see verse 2) to see themselves as the older son. What was the older son – and by implication the Pharisees – missing out on?

4 How can we make sure we don't miss out in the same way?

The Parable of the Lost Son is a wonderful picture of the compassion of God and the mission of Jesus.

> *Thank God for the extraordinary nature of his fatherly compassion for you. Who do you need to have compassion on in your daily life? Pray about this and ask God to give you his compassion for them.*

DAY 4

> *Read Colossians 1:15–23.*

This letter was written by Paul to the church in Colosse, and these verses give us a profound insight into who Jesus is.

1 **What does Paul mean when he calls Jesus "the image of the invisible God"? (see verse 19)**

2 **Paul also describes Jesus as "the firstborn over all creation". What does he mean by that, according to verses 16–18?**

3 **Jesus is described by Paul as the one who reveals God, creator of the universe, the purpose of the universe, the sustainer of everything, the head of the church and the reconciler. Identify the verses that correspond to these descriptions.**

4 **In the light of this, what should our attitude be towards Jesus?**

continued »

5 Because of humankind's rebellion against God (Genesis 3), everything has been severed from its rightful relationship with the Father and needs to be reconciled to him. How is this achieved? (see verse 20)

6 Verse 22 mentions our own reconciliation with Jesus. For what purpose have we been reconciled?

7 According to verse 23, what should our response be to this reconciliation?

> *Reflect on the descriptions of Jesus you found in question 3, and praise God for such a mighty Saviour. Pray too that you will "continue in your faith, established and firm, not moved from the hope held out in the gospel."*

DAY 5

> *Re-read the Bible passages you've read over the past week. Choose a verse that you found particularly helpful, write it down in the space below and memorize it.*

DAY 6

> *Read Philippians 2:12–30 in preparation for* **Discipleship Explored**.

WEEK 4
TRANSFORMED BY CHRIST

GROUP DISCUSSION 1

> Ask participants to turn to Week 4 on page 25 of their Study Guide.

> Ask if anyone has any questions arising from last week's studies and discuss as necessary.

> Ask participants to turn to Philippians 2:5–11. A leader – or one of the participants – should read the passage aloud and the group should then work through the study below. The answers are printed here for your reference.

1 Our attitude "should be the same as that of Christ Jesus" (verse 5). What exactly was Jesus' attitude? (see verses 7–8)

He made himself nothing, became like a servant, humbled himself, and became obedient to death, even death on a cross.

2 Jesus "did not consider equality with God something to be grasped". Why? (see verse 6)

He is already God.

3 Are there any situations in which a Christian needs to "grasp equality with God"? Why or why not?

There are no situations in which a Christian needs to do this. After all, "grasping equality with God" is practically the definition of sin. Moreover, just as Jesus had everything because he is God, so we have everything in Christ. That means we don't need to live self-centred, "grasping" lives.

continued

4 What were the results of Jesus' attitude, according to verses 9–11?

God exalted him to the highest place and gave him the name that is above every name, that every knee should bow to Jesus, acknowledging that he is Lord, to the glory of God.

5 Having read this passage, how can you live "to the glory of God" (verse 11) this week?

It might be helpful to look at 1 Corinthians 10:31.

TALK   **PHILIPPIANS 2:12–30**

Additional notes for leaders:

Work out your salvation (v12) – note that Paul does not say "work for your salvation". Salvation has already been bought by Christ's death. Paul's phrase alludes to the way in which we live in the light of that salvation.

Fear (v12) – Exodus 14:31 might help you to explain what it means to "fear" God. The Israelites saw the awe-inspiring power of God, which led them to fear God and so they put their trust in him. See also Jesus' words in Luke 12:4–7.

Shine like stars (v15) – this is not just about "living a distinctive life", as Paul makes clear in the next verse. The way we "shine like stars" is by holding out the word of life. (see also Daniel 12:3)

1 Was there anything in the talk you didn't understand, you disagree with or that you found particularly interesting?

2 In your own words, what does Paul command in verse 12?

3 What will it mean in practice for you to "work out your salvation with fear and trembling"?

4 After the challenge of verse 12, why should Paul's next words inspire confidence in his readers?

5 In what ways are you aware of God transforming you or other Christians you know?

6 According to verses 15 and 16, what makes us "shine like stars"?

7 Which do you think is more necessary: to tell people the gospel or to live a godly life among them? Why?

WEEK 4

THE WEEK AHEAD

In Philippians 2:12–13, Paul tells the Philippian church to "work out" their salvation. The studies this week explore what that means.

SUNDAY

> Read the passage that will be preached at the church service you attend.

On the other six days...

DAY 1

> Re-read Philippians 2:12–30 and think about the answers you gave to the questions in GROUP DISCUSSION 2 on the previous page.

> Pray that you would be able to "work out your salvation with fear and trembling", thanking God that he is at work in you.

DAY 2

> Read Luke 14:25–33.

In this passage, Jesus explains what it will cost to follow him. It is significant that Jesus is addressing the large crowd who have been travelling with him; he wants them to understand that there is a big difference between being a true follower and just being a spectator.

When Jesus uses the word "hate", he is not telling us, for example, to abandon the commandment to "honour your father and your mother" (Exodus 20:12). He uses the word to show the radical nature of following him. We must always put Christ first.

continued »

1 What is involved in being a follower of Jesus, according to verses 26–27?

2 What does this say about who Jesus is, if we are to love him more than anything or anyone else?

3 What is the similarity between the man in verses 28–30 and the king in verses 31–32? In what way are they different?

4 What is the point Jesus is making with these two stories? (see verse 33)

> Pray that you will become more and more single-minded in following Jesus.

> *Read Galatians 5:16–26.*

In this letter, Paul is writing to the churches in Galatia. His main point in these verses is that there is a conflict between the Spirit and the sinful nature in every Christian's life.

1 **There is an important balance in verses 16–18. The desires we have lead us in one of two directions. Our aim should be to cooperate with the Holy Spirit and feed that part of our lives, starving the sinful side of us. In what areas of your life do you feel the most conflict?**

2 **Looking at verses 19–21, are there any things mentioned here which you need to turn from and ask forgiveness for?**

(Note: Some things are obvious actions but others are attitudes that are easier to hide.)

3 **Looking at "the fruit of the Spirit" in verses 22 and 23, which qualities do you particularly need to develop?**

4 **Paul tells us to "keep in step" with the Spirit (verse 25). How can you do this, according to the verses you've just read?**

continued »

Although it is important that we are aware of the areas in our lives where we need to change, it is also very important that we don't become weighed down by a sense of insurmountable guilt. Remember, God's acceptance of us is based on what Jesus has done, not on what we have done.

> Thank God that "if we confess our sins, he is faithful and just and will forgive us our sins and purify us from all unrighteousness" (1 John 1:9).

DAY 4

> Read Romans 12:1–13.

This letter was written by Paul to the church in Rome. The "therefore" in 12:1 follows on from the first eleven chapters of Romans, which were a comprehensive explanation of the gospel. In chapter 12, Paul lays out the practical implications the gospel should have on our lives.

1 **What does verse 1 say about what worship is?**

2 **How is this different to simply singing hymns at church on Sunday?**

3 **What is the motivation for being "living sacrifices"? (see verse 1)**

4 **Verse 2 suggests that our whole way of thinking should change. What will be the result of this change?**

continued >>

5 Verses 3–8 are about using our gifts in the church. In what ways are you currently doing this?

(Note: The list Paul gives in verses 6–8 is not exhaustive.)

6 In verses 9–13 Paul tells us how Christians should behave towards one another. What are these qualities?

Verses 9–13 are very practical. Remembering the sacrificial love of God enables us to understand how we should love and serve others.

⟩ *Pray through these verses, asking that God would increase your "devotion" and "brotherly love" towards other Christians.*

DAY 5

⟩ *Re-read the Bible passages you've read over the past week. Choose a verse that you found particularly helpful, write it down in the space below and memorize it.*

DAY 6

⟩ *Read Philippians 3:1–9 in preparation for* **Discipleship Explored**.

WEEK 5
RIGHTEOUS IN CHRIST

GROUP DISCUSSION 1

> Ask participants to turn to Week 5 on page 33 of their Study Guide.

> Ask if anyone has any questions arising from last week's studies and discuss as necessary.

> Ask participants to turn to Philippians 2:19–30. A leader – or one of the participants – should read the passage aloud and the group should then work through the study below. The answers are printed here for your reference.

1 What plans for the future does Paul outline? (see verses 19, 24, 25 and compare with Philippians 1:21–24)

To send Timothy to Philippi; to visit them himself; to send Epaphroditus back to them. Remember that Paul doesn't know whether he's going to live or die (see Philippians 1:21–24), but he still keeps on living for God, working out his salvation.

2 What do we learn about Timothy and his priorities from these verses?

He has a genuine interest in other people's welfare. His character is proven; he is faithful. He has a close relationship with Paul. He is servant-hearted and works for the gospel.

3 How does Paul describe Epaphroditus and what insight do we get into Epaphroditus' attitude and motivation?

He is a "brother" (i.e. Christian); "fellow-worker" (i.e. works with other Christians); "fellow-soldier" (i.e. contends for the gospel). He is selfless: even when facing extreme illness and at the point of death, Epaphroditus was more concerned about how others felt when they heard he was ill than about his own illness. He "almost died for the work of Christ"; he was willing even to risk his life for the sake of the gospel.

continued >>

WEEK 5

4 Why do you think Paul mentions these two men at this point in his letter? (see Philippians 2:4–5)

Paul isn't just telling the Philippians his future plans. He wants the Philippians to learn from these two men. Both are examples of Christ-like service (the lesson Paul has been teaching in 2:1–18). Both put the interests of Christ – and therefore of others – before their own interests.

5 Paul, Timothy and Epaphroditus all demonstrated their genuine care for fellow believers. In what practical ways can we also do this?

This question is designed to help participants apply what they have learned.

TALK   PHILIPPIANS 3:1–9

Additional notes for leaders:

Watch out (v2) – the phrase is repeated three times in the Greek. Paul aims to keep them alert, such is the danger of false teaching.

We... are the circumcision (v3) – if false teachers were trying to make Gentile Christians adopt Jewish rituals, they were effectively claiming to be "the true circumcision" (God's chosen ones). Paul refutes this. See also Romans 2:28–29.

Righteousness (v9) – the standard of goodness required to be right with God. This standard is perfection and sinlessness. Only Christ has ever achieved this standard.

1 Was there anything in the talk you didn't understand, you disagree with or that you found particularly interesting?

2 Paul lists his impressive religious credentials in verses 5–6. What similar things do people today think will make them right with God?

3 How had Paul's attitude changed and why? (see verses 7 and 8)

4 What does it mean for us as Christians to "consider everything a loss..."?

5 Verse 9 explains what "knowing" or "gaining" Christ means. How would you paraphrase verse 9 to explain it to one of your non-Christian friends?

6 What does reliance on oneself show about our view of Jesus Christ?

THE WEEK AHEAD

In Philippians 3:9, Paul speaks about a righteousness that comes as a gift from God and which can be ours through faith. The studies this week explore that theme.

SUNDAY

> Read the passage that will be preached at the church service you attend.

On the other six days...

DAY 1

> Re-read Philippians 3:1–9 and think about the answers you gave to the questions in GROUP DISCUSSION 2 on the previous page.

> Thank God that you have a "righteousness that comes from God and is by faith".

DAY 2

> Re-read Ephesians 2:1–10.

You may remember that we explored part of this passage in Week 1. These verses contain an overview of our salvation.

1 What was our condition before we became Christians? (see verses 1–3)

continued

2 Why did God do something about our condition? (see verse 4)

3 Look at your answer to question 1. In what ways did we deserve God's love? (see also Romans 5:8)

4 So what does Paul mean when he says "it is by grace you have been saved" (verse 5)?

5 Why is the distinction between works (verse 9) and faith (verse 8) important to understand?

> *Pray that you will gain an even clearer understanding of God's grace, so that you can live in the light of it.*

> *Read Romans 3:20–26.*

This is one of the most extraordinary passages in the New Testament about what God has done for us through Christ's death.

1 What does "the law" do, according to verse 20?

2 According to the same verse, what will observing the law not do?

3 The word "justification" means being declared "not guilty". How can we, who are guilty, be justified? (see verse 24)

4 How does this demonstrate both God's justice and his love? (see verses 25–26)

> *Give thanks to God for his justice and for his love, demonstrated by Jesus' death.*

DAY 4

> *Read Romans 5:1–11.*

In these verses Paul describes the peace and joy that come from being justified.

1 What six statements are true of all whom God has justified?

(Clue: The first is in verse 1, the second and third are in verse 2, the fourth in verse 3, the fifth in verse 9, the last in verse 11.)

2 What impact should each of these truths have on your life?

3 According to Paul, what should be our attitude to suffering? Why? (see verses 3–5)

continued »

4 How can we be sure of God's love, according to Paul? (see verses 5 and 8)

5 Why is the "right answer" to the question "Have you been saved?" both "Yes" and "No"? (see verses 9–10)

> *Thank God for the peace you have with him, his presence in your life through the Holy Spirit and the hope of future glory.*

DAY 5

> *Re-read the Bible passages you've read over the past week. Choose a verse that you found particularly helpful, write it down in the space below and memorize it.*

DAY 6

> *Read Philippians 3:10 – 4:1 in preparation for **Discipleship Explored**.*

WEEK 6
KNOWING CHRIST

GROUP DISCUSSION 1

> Ask participants to turn to Week 6 on page 41 of their Study Guide.

> Ask if anyone has any questions arising from last week's studies and discuss as necessary.

> Ask participants to turn to Philippians 3:1–4. A leader – or one of the participants – should read the passage aloud and the group should then work through the study below. The answers are printed here for your reference.

---

1 Why do the Philippians need a safeguard? (see verses 1 and 2)

They were in danger. Paul's words were vital to keep them alert and watchful for the danger of false teaching.

2 Some people were teaching that physical circumcision is necessary. Why does Paul say that Christians "are the circumcision"? (see also Romans 2:28–29)

Remember from last week that nothing that we do makes us right with God. Romans 2 reminds us that it is our hearts that make us unacceptable to God and only the Holy Spirit can change our hearts. This change is what Paul refers to as true circumcision.

3 What other marks of the true believer does Paul mention in verse 3?

Paul says that believers: "worship by the Spirit of God" (i.e. that the whole of their lives are directed by the Holy Spirit); "glory in Christ Jesus" (i.e. rejoice in Jesus and all that he has done for them); "put no confidence in the flesh" (i.e. don't depend on anything they have done to make them right with God).

continued

4 Paul wanted the Philippians to put their confidence in Jesus and in nothing else. Why are Christians sometimes tempted to put their confidence in additional things?

It is often hard to trust that we can be saved and live by grace alone. Sometimes it feels more comfortable to rely on our own actions as a measure of how right we are with God.

5 What things can we be tempted to rely on in addition to our confidence in Jesus?

How often we read the Bible, how earnestly we pray, how many people we tell about Jesus and so on.

6 What should we remember when we are tempted to place confidence in these additional things?

Philippians 3:9 may help participants to phrase an answer.

TALK   PHILIPPIANS 3:10 – 4:1

Additional notes for leaders:

All of us who are mature... (v15) – mature Christians know that they constantly need to press on to know Jesus better. In a way, maturity means knowing that you are immature.

Earthly things (v19) – note that Paul says "earthly things" not "wicked things". Although people's minds may be on things that are not "bad" in themselves, these things may nevertheless distract them from focusing on Christ.

Citizenship is in heaven (v20) – it may be helpful to look at 1 Corinthians 7:29–31 and 1 Peter 2:11.

1 Was there anything in the talk you didn't understand, you disagree with or that you found particularly interesting?

2 In your own words, what is the "one thing" Paul does (according to verses 12–14) and why?

3 From verses 12–16 what might hinder us from pressing on? What should encourage us to keep pressing on?

4 In verse 16 Paul says "let us live up to what we have already attained". The example of others can help us do this. Why is it important to choose the right role-models? (see verses 17–19)

5 Look at the phrases in verse 19 that describe those who are "enemies of the cross of Christ". How do people behave in these ways today?

6 What are the sharp contrasts between the descriptions in verse 19 and those in verses 20–21?

7 What does it mean for you to know in your daily life that your "citizenship is in heaven" and that Christ will return?

THE WEEK AHEAD

In Philippians 3:12–14, Paul declares his determination to "press on" as a Christian. The studies this week will help you think about how you can "press on".

SUNDAY

> Read the passage that will be preached at the church service you attend.

On the other six days...

DAY 1

> Re-read Philippians 3:10 – 4:1 and think about the answers you gave to the questions in GROUP DISCUSSION 2 on the previous page.

> Pray that you would be able to keep your focus completely on Jesus Christ.

DAY 2

> Read Matthew 6:19–24.

These verses are part of Jesus' preaching referred to as the "Sermon on the Mount".

1 Jesus tells us to store up "treasures in heaven" rather than "treasures on earth". Why? (see verses 19–20)

continued »

2 What does Jesus mean when he says: "For where your treasure is, there your heart will be also" (verse 21)?

3 How do you invest your time and energy, and what does this show about where your heart is?

4 Jesus says in verse 24 that no-one can serve two masters. What competes in your life with serving Jesus?

5 What should you do about that?

> *Ask God to help you choose treasures that will endure through eternity.*

> *Read Matthew 6:25–34.*

This passage carries on from Day 2's reading.

1 What do you learn about God's love for you from verses 26 and 30?

2 According to verse 32, why shouldn't we worry about food or drink or clothing?

3 What should we do instead, according to verse 33?

4 In what practical ways can we do that?

> *Pray that you would be able to trust God and depend on him for everything.*

> *Read Matthew 7:24–29.*

This parable concludes the Sermon on the Mount.

1 There are two men in this parable – how are they described?

2 There is a similarity and a difference between the two householders – what are they?

3 There are two foundations in this parable – what is the difference between them?

4 There are two consequences in this parable – how are they described?

continued »

5 What does the storm in verses 25 and 27 symbolize? (see also verses 13, 19 and 23)

6 Is it enough to listen to Jesus' words? Why or why not?

> *Pray about the areas of your life where you can put into practice what Jesus teaches here.*

DAY 5

> *Re-read the Bible passages you've read over the past week. Choose a verse that you found particularly helpful, write it down in the space below and memorize it.*

DAY 6

> *Read Philippians 4:2–9 in preparation for* **Discipleship Explored**.

WEEK 7
REJOICING IN CHRIST

GROUP DISCUSSION 1

▷ *Ask participants to turn to Week 7 on page 49 of their Study Guide.*

▷ *Ask if anyone has any questions arising from last week's studies and discuss as necessary.*

▷ *Ask participants to turn to Philippians 3:10–11. A leader – or one of the participants – should read the passage aloud and the group should then work through the study below. The answers are printed here for your reference.*

1 In verse 10, Paul says that his goal is "to know Christ". From verses 10 and 11, what challenge arises from knowing Christ?

We will "share in his sufferings".
Knowing Christ results in us facing suffering for the sake of Christ.
Note: 1 Peter 4:12–16 may be helpful.

2 From verses 10 and 11, what comforts arise from knowing Christ?

We will know "the power of his resurrection".
We will also "attain to the resurrection of the dead"; in other words, when we die we will be resurrected to be with Christ.
Note: see also Philippians 3:21.

3 What does Paul mean by wanting to know "the power of his resurrection"? (see also Ephesians 1:17–20)

He wants to know the power that raised Christ from the dead in his own life. It is amazing to know that the same divine force that raised Jesus from the dead is at work in us.

4 Can you echo Paul's words in these verses? Why or why not?

This question is designed to help participants apply what they have learned.

Additional notes for leaders:

Rejoice in the Lord (v4) – in Philippians we see Paul's joy (1:4, 18; 2:2, 17, 18 etc), despite being in prison (1:13). It may also be useful to look at Habakkuk 3:17–18 where joy "in the Lord" is possible, regardless of circumstances.

The Lord is near (v5) – near in the sense that he is with us by his Spirit but also in the sense that Christ will return (see Philippians 3:20).

Think about such things (v8) – has the sense of "ponder" or "dwell upon"; in other words, "take time to think about".

GROUP DISCUSSION 2

1 Was there anything in the talk you didn't understand, you disagree with or that you found particularly interesting?

2 Do you think Paul is being unrealistic to say "rejoice in the Lord always" (verse 4)? Why or why not?

3 When we find it hard to rejoice, what practical steps can we take to help us "rejoice always"?

4 Why will knowing that "the Lord is near" (verse 5) enable us to be gentle?

5 What action should we take when we are anxious, and why? (see verses 6–7)

6 What does it mean to pray "with thanksgiving" (verse 6) and what does this help us to guard against?

THE WEEK AHEAD

The studies this week will help you find out more about prayer.

SUNDAY

> *Read the passage that will be preached at the church service you attend.*

On the other six days...

DAY 1

> *Re-read Philippians 4:2–9 and think about the answers you gave to the questions in GROUP DISCUSSION 2 on the previous page.*

> *Remembering verse 6, pray about the things that make you anxious.*

DAY 2

> *Read Matthew 6:5–15.*

Jesus teaches his disciples about prayer.

1 In verses 5–8, what contrasts are there between hypocritical or pagan prayer and the prayer Jesus urges us to engage in?

2 What is Jesus emphasizing about the father-child relationship in verses 5–8?

(Note: Notice how often Jesus uses the word "Father".)

continued

3 We pray to our heavenly Father (verse 9). What are the first things that Jesus tells the disciples to pray? (see verses 9–10)

(Note: "hallowed" means "revered" or "honoured".)

4 Why should we pray for these things first?

5 Go through the rest of the prayer phrase by phrase. What is Jesus teaching us about prayer in each phrase?

6 Look at Jesus' conclusion in verses 14 and 15. If our lives are not characterized by forgiveness, what might that suggest about our relationship with God?

> *Use Jesus' prayer as a model for your own prayer.*

DAY 3

> *Read Colossians 1:3–14.*

Paul is writing from prison to the church in Colosse.

1 What does Paul thank God for when he prays for the Colossians? (see verses 3–4)

2 Where does the Colossians' faith and love come from? (see verse 5)

3 What is the main thing Paul prays for the Colossians? (see verse 9)

4 Why does he pray for this? (see verses 10–12)

> *Think of Christians you would like to pray for and use these verses as a model for your prayers.*

DAY 4

> *Read Colossians 4:2–6.*

Here we get an insight into the prayers Paul would like prayed for him.

1 What do we learn from verse 2 about the way we should pray?

2 Given the reason that Paul is in prison (see the end of verse 3), why is Paul's request in verse 3 surprising?

3 How can verses 3 and 4 help you pray for other Christians who want to tell their friends about Jesus?

4 What advice does Paul give about how we should act towards non-Christians? (see verses 5 and 6)

> *Pray for your effectiveness, and the effectiveness of others, in proclaiming the gospel.*

DAY 5

> Re-read the Bible passages you've read over the past week. Choose a verse that you found particularly helpful, write it down in the space below and memorize it.

DAY 6

> Read Philippians 4:10–23 in preparation for **Discipleship Explored**.

WEEK 8
CONTENT IN CHRIST

GROUP DISCUSSION 1

 Ask participants to turn to Week 8 on page 57 of their Study Guide.

 Ask if anyone has any questions arising from last week's studies and discuss as necessary.

 Ask participants to turn to Philippians 4:8–9. A leader – or one of the participants – should read the passage aloud and the group should then work through the study below. The answers are printed here for your reference.

1 What should we spend our time thinking about, according to verse 8?

Whatever is: true, noble, right, pure, lovely, admirable. All of which are summarized by – "if anything is excellent or praiseworthy".

2 Write down the opposite of all the descriptive words Paul uses in verse 8. If you were to dwell on such things, what effect would it have on you?

False, depraved, wrong, tainted, ugly, shameful. This question aims to show that what we reflect upon has an effect on how we behave.

3 On a typical day, what things tend to preoccupy our minds?

Obvious examples include: TV, newspapers, internet, friends, films.

Note: The impact of these things may not necessarily be negative, it is a question of learning to "discern what is best" (1:10).

continued »

WEEK 8

4 What incentive is there to do what Paul says? (see verse 9)

If we aim to follow Paul's example (as he followed the example of Jesus; 1 Corinthians 11:1), the God of peace will be with us. When we live obedient lives we experience God's peace in our lives.

5 How will you act upon Paul's command in verse 8?

Encourage your group to think creatively and practically about what Paul means here when he talks about "excellent or praiseworthy" things. These may include – but are certainly not limited to – the glorious truths contained in God's word, the natural beauty of God's creation, godly virtues in other people, and so on.

TALK   PHILIPPIANS 4:10–23

Additional notes for leaders:

I know what it is to be in need... (v12) – it might be worth reading through 2 Corinthians 11:23–29 to help the group see how Paul suffered as a result of preaching the gospel.

I can do everything (v13) – refers to facing the situations which Paul has mentioned in verse 12: hunger, plenty. It does not mean that God will give us strength to achieve anything we set our minds to doing. It is about being content whatever the circumstances.

Credited to your account (v17) – this does not mean we can attain righteousness ourselves. The phrase carries the idea of "fruit" (as in 1:11) – the result of God's work in us, after salvation.

1 Was there anything in the talk you didn't understand, you disagree with or that you found particularly interesting?

2 In what ways does society tempt us to be discontent?

3 Paul says that he has "learned the secret of being content in any and every situation". Where does Paul find true contentment, according to verse 13? (see also 4:7–9; 1:21; 3:10–11)

4 What practical steps can you take in order to be content in "any and every situation"?

5 What do verses 14–18 tell us about the Philippians' generosity?

6 How should we "share in the troubles" of fellow Christians today?

7 Does verse 19 mean that Christians will never be in financial difficulty? Why or why not?

8 What is encouraging about the way Paul ends his letter? (see verses 20–23)

THE WEEK AHEAD

Paul ends his letter to the Philippians by speaking about contentment. The studies this week will help you to see how this is possible.

SUNDAY

> *Read the passage that will be preached at the church service you attend.*

On the other six days...

DAY 1

> *Re-read Philippians 4:10–23 and think about the answers you gave to the questions in GROUP DISCUSSION 2 on the previous page.*

> *Pray that you would learn to be "content in any and every situation".*

DAY 2

> *Read Hebrews 4:14–16.*

This short passage gives us great assurance.

1 Why should we hold "firmly" to the faith we profess (verse 14)?

2 What do you consider to be your particular weaknesses and temptations (verse 15)?

continued »

3 **What should we do in times of weakness and temptation? (see verses 15–16)**

4 **How will God respond if we do this? (see verse 16)**

> Use your answers to these questions to help you pray.

DAY 3

> Read 1 Timothy 1:12–17.

Paul wrote two letters to his younger colleague Timothy. Here Paul talks about his sense of unworthiness because he used to persecute the church.

1 **What does Paul thank Jesus for in verse 12?**

2 **What did Paul receive from Jesus, according to verse 14?**

continued »

3　Why is the "saying" in verse 15 so fundamental for Paul and for us?

4　How was Paul's life an example of God's patience? (see verses 13 and 16)

5　How is your life an example of God's patience to those who aren't yet Christians? (see verse 16)

6　In verse 12, Paul mentions that Jesus gave him strength. In what ways have you too received strength from Jesus?

> *Pray about your witness as a Christian in the places you work and live. Ask for God's strength in your witness.*

DAY 4

> Read Ephesians 3:14–21.

This prayer is right in the middle of Paul's letter to the Ephesians. In it, he prays that they would have "power".

1 What is the first thing Paul prays for the Ephesians? (see verses 16–17a)

2 What is required from the Ephesians to make this prayer effective (verse 17a)?

3 Given that the Ephesians are already Christians, and therefore already have Christ living in them, what does Paul mean when he prays that Christ would "dwell" in them?

continued »

4 What is the second thing Paul prays for the Ephesians? (see verses 17b–19)

5 How can the "love" that Paul mentions in verse 19 be known, but at the same time "surpass knowledge"?

6 What is it about the end of Paul's prayer that encourages us to pray? (see verse 20)

> Using these verses, pray for yourself and the church as a whole, that we would grow in our knowledge of the love of Jesus.

DAY 5

> Re-read the Bible passages you've read over the past week. Choose a verse that you found particularly helpful, write it down in the space below and memorize it.

> *Now that you've finished* **Discipleship Explored**, *spend some time writing down the things you have learned. Pray that you would be able to put them into practice.*

continued

DISCIPLESHIP EXPLORED
THE WEEKS AHEAD

> *Don't forget to support your participants now that the course is over (see "After the Course" in Section 2 of this book). The following appears in the participant's* Study Guide *and is included for your reference.*

Paul wants the Philippians to experience "progress and joy in the faith" and our prayer for you is the same.

With this in mind, it's a good idea to join a group that meets regularly to study the Bible. You will also want to continue your own daily Bible reading. (The book of James is a great follow-up to **Discipleship Explored**.)

The website www.discipleshipexplored.org also has a recommended reading section that you may find useful.

"Finally... whatever is true, whatever is noble, whatever is right, whatever is pure, whatever is lovely, whatever is admirable – if anything is excellent or praiseworthy – think about such things."

Discipleship Explored was developed by Barry Cooper, Rupert Higgins, Sam Shammas and Katy Walton.

The course has been greatly enhanced by the contributions of Diane Bainbridge, James Burstow, Anita Harlock, Charmaine Muir, Jackie Sieling, Tim Thornborough, Anne Woodcock, the DE leaders at All Souls Church, and the many other churches who graciously offered feedback as they trialled the material.

ACKNOWLEDGEMENTS